THE NATIONAL TRUST

Investigating Myths and Legends

By Alison Honey
Illustrated by Merida Woodford

Contents

National Trust Myths and Legends

The Myths and legends in this book are all connected with buildings or land looked after by the National Trust. Some tales are very, very old, while others are more up to date and are newcomers to the folklore and legends of Britain. It's up to you to decide how many are true!

Ever-changing Tales

Many of the myths and legends which you will read about in this book are hundreds of years old and have been passed on from generation to generation, told as stories or even sung as ballads. You may recognise some of them or think that some sound only slightly familiar.

Have you ever played Chinese Whispers, the game where you sit round in a ring and whisper a phrase quickly in you neighbour's ear? They then repeat what they thought they heard to the person next to them and so on until the last person says out loud the phrase which they finally heard. Often the sentence at the end is completely different to what you started with.

It can sometimes be the same with myths and legends. Most of them go back to ages before most people could read or write and so stories would be passed on by word of mouth. Each time the tale was told it would be slightly different as every storyteller would have an individual style so that over the years the original story might end up very different.

Worldly Wonders

Myths and legends are part of the ancient tradition of storytelling which has played, and still plays, an important role in the life of communities throughout the whole world. It's difficult for us to imagine a life without television, radio, cinema, videos, books and newspapers, but when some of the tales in this book began, people got their entertainment from storytellers and singers.

For thousands of years, people the world over have passed long evenings and long journeys listening to incredible tales told by skilled storytellers and these have been passed down to us over the generations. Many of the same mythical creatures appear in tales from countries thousands of miles apart: you'll find tales about dragons in China as well as Europe; monstrous dogs crop up in Australian Aboriginal myths just as they do in British Celtic folk tales, while just about every culture world-wide seems to have its favourite ghost stories.

MONSTROUS DOG

Myth or legend

As a general rule myths are what we would think of as fairy tales - stories about giants, dragons, fairies and fabulous beasts - while legends are tales about 'real' people like King Arthur and Robin Hood. However, legends have usually become so exaggerated as they have been told over and over again, that they reach us in a very different form. The legend of King Arthur and his Knights of the Holy Grail has certainly come a long way from the real story of the fifth century British leader, to the many twentieth century versions.

The land and buildings owned and cared for by the National Trust are full of such legends and myths. Now you know a little more about them and how they began, turn the page and sample some for yourself...

THE NATIONAL TRUST

Fee, Fi, Fo, Fum...

Many giants have stamped their enormous footprints across land now cared for by the National Trust. Here are just a few...

The Giant of St Michael's Mount

Long, long ago on an island off the coast of Cornwall, lived an evil giant called Cormoran. He stood as tall as two houses and his eyes were the colour of a muddy sea after a storm. The old leather boots he wore were made from the hide of ten cows and were coated in slimy, rotting seaweed. His mouth was ringed with dried blood from eating sheep stolen from the flocks of the poor villagers across the bay. His roar terrified the local people who ran into their houses and locked their doors as soon as they heard him crashing and splashing through the sea in search of food.

One of the villagers was a widow who lived with her son Jack. The little money they had came from selling the milk, cheese and butter which came from their only cow and the widow was terrified that one day the giant would steal the animal. Daily, Jack saw his mother grow ill with worry and he knew that he had to get rid of the giant once and for all. One night, when he heard Cormoran's snoring, he took a spade, a horn and an axe and rowed his tiny boat across the moon-shimmering sea to the Mount.

By the light of the moon he began to dig a hole in the path which led up to the giant's castle. At first it was no bigger than a football, then as he dug it grew to the size of a barrel, then a cart and the harder he worked the deeper the hole became until it measured the depth of two houses.

Covering his trap with branches and straw, he hid behind a rock, put the horn to his mouth and blew until the night air was filled with its deep sound. Suddenly the giant's snoring stopped and Cormoran let out a bellowing, angry roar as he was woken from his sleep. As Cormoran thundered down the hill, Jack felt the ground shaking like an earthquake and then he heard a blood-curdling cry as the giant fell through the branches into the trap. Rushing from his hiding place, Jack took his axe, raised it above his head and brought it crashing down on Cormoran's head.

When Jack returned to the mainland and told the villagers that the giant was dead, they were so pleased that they gave him a reward so that he and his mother never had to worry about money again.

Giant's Causeway

On the North coast of Ireland is a strange rock formation of hexagonal columns stretching from the cliffs into the sea, called the Giant's Causeway. There are similar rocks at Staffa on the west coast of Scotland.

Many years ago the Irish giant, Finn McCool, decided to build a causeway across the sea in order to fight his enemy, the giant Bennan Donner, in Scotland. Finn lost the battle and fled back to North Antrim across the Causeway destroying most of it behind him to stop Bennan Donner following him - leaving only a trail of the hexagonal blocks leading into the sea.

Another version of the story tells of Finn dressing up as a baby and lying in wait for Bennan Donner. The Scottish giant strides across the Causeway, sees the enormous 'baby' and turns tail in terror at the thought of the size of the father.

The hexagonal basalt columns of the Giant's Causeway are the result of volcanic activity 60 million years ago. All around this stretch of coastline the columns form strange shapes and many have been given names to match, such as the Giant's Boot, the Giant's Granny and the Giant's Eye. There is also a Wishing Chair formed out of the stones - sit in it, make a wish and see if your dreams come true!

Gentle giants

Not all giants were fierce. At Carn Galver in Cornwall lived a giant who protected the people of Morvah and Zennor from hostile giants in return for food. The 66-ton Logan Rock which balances on a cliff east of Porthcurno was said to have been built by the giant to rock himself to sleep. It was always assumed that although the boulder rocked it would never actually fall until, in 1824, a sailor called Lt Goldsmith, proved otherwise by pushing it until it fell off the cliff onto the beach below. He should have thought twice before pushing – as a punishment he was forced to replace the rock at his own expense.

A Real Giant

At Speke Hall in Merseyside you can see the picture of a real life giant - the so-called Child of Hale, John Middleton, who lived from 1578 to 1623 and was 9ft 3in tall. The story goes that he had been a normal size until he fell asleep on the beach one evening, was bewitched and woke up to find that he'd grown to an enormous height. Middleton's fame spread and James I invited him to Court to fight his champion wrestler. Middleton defeated him effortlessly. Another story which reveals his amazing strength tells of Middleton being attacked by a bull one day - he simply grabbed the poor animal by its horns and threw it over a nearby hedge.

Strange stones

A ll over the United Kingdom there are strange standing stones dating back thousands of years and still surrounded by mystery. There are various theories surrounding these stone arrangements which claim that they are sacred sites connected with ancient religions and some even suggest that human sacrifices took place. However, no one can be sure of their exact role. Apart from the archaeological theories there are, not surprisingly, a few tales of how the stones got there in the first place....

The Giants' Dance

Stonehenge in Wiltshire must be one of the most famous historic sites in England. Tests have shown that the huge stones which make up Stonehenge came from the Prescelly Mountains in South Wales over 4000 years ago and each of the sixty stones weighs over four tons. No one knows exactly how or why the stones could have been brought all that way from Wales to Wiltshire. It would be difficult enough today. How do you think it could have been done without modern machinery? Legend has it that they originally came from Africa and were taken to Ireland by a race of giants where the arrangement was known as the 'Dance of the Giants'. They were then brought across to Salisbury Plain by the Wizard Merlin who used his magical powers to fly them across the sea.

A Stone Army

The Bronze Age Rollright Stones in Oxfordshire are said to be uncountable - no one has ever arrived at the same number of stones three times running! According to legend, the stones are a bewitched army which was turned to stone and is waiting for the curse to be broken. Anyone who tries to move or damage the stones is plagued by bad luck. Many other stone circles are rumoured to be human figures turned to stone - usually as a punishment for doing something wrong such as dancing on a Sunday.

Another stone circle to visit is Castlerigg Stone Circle in Cumbria. What do you think all these different strange stones were used for?

Avebury

There are stone circles, consisting of nearly 100 stones, at Avebury in Wiltshire. These were also built 4,000 years ago and weigh up to 60 tons each. They were probably erected for use in mysterious pagan ceremonies but as with all things that old, there is no recorded information to tell us about them so there is a great deal of detective work required.

In the Middle Ages the Church became worried that people were turning away from Christianity to Paganism again. The Church ordered that the stones should be buried - quite a task. In 1938 a skeleton of a man who had died around 1320, was discovered underneath one of the stones - he was probably crushed to death in his attempts at trying to bury the stone. Luckily the idea of burying the stones was soon abandoned but centuries later the site faced a different threat when local farmers used the stones for various building works. After much detective work earlier this century most of the original stones were tracked down and replaced.

Hill figures

A t several places on the chalk downs of Southern England you can find enormous figures cut into the hillsides. You can walk round most of them but they are best seen from a distance or from the air. Why and when they were carved is often a mystery but local legends provide a few solutions.

The Cerne Giant

On the chalk downs above Cerne Abbas in Dorset is a huge figure of a naked giant, waving a club carved out of the hillside. It probably dates back a couple of thousand years but mystery surrounds the 55m tall figure. One legend is that a giant was terrorising the area, raiding farmers' flocks, but was killed by a brave band of local villagers. Where the giant's body fell on the hillside, the brave villagers cut around his shape, leaving his outline in the chalk as a warning to other giants to stay away. Another theory is that the chalk figure is Hercules.

The Vale of the White Horse

On the downs at Uffington in Oxfordshire is a figure of a white horse carved out of the chalk on the hillside below the Celtic hill fort. Archaeologists believe it was carved about 3,000 years ago during the Iron Age on an important site for burials. The horse was a sacred figure for the Celts and many of their gods were connected with animals such as the goddess Epona, who was also responsible for protecting the dead.

There are many stories surrounding this strange figure - which doesn't really look like a horse at all. Some say that at night it gets up and goes to a nearby valley, known as The Manger, to feed. This is not the only legend attached to this area. Not far away from the White Horse is an empty iron age burial mound known as Wayland's Smithy. Wayland was the blacksmith to the Norse gods and when Christianity came to Britain he was put out of a job, so had to resort to shoeing the horses of mere mortals. It is said that if you leave your horse and a coin inside the barrow, the horse will be shod when you get back.

Nearby is Dragon Hill where legend tells us St George killed the dragon - it has a bald patch where the dragon's blood fell and nothing has grown since.

Other hill figures to see:

The Long Man of Wilmington, East Sussex (probably Iron Age)

Whipsnade White Horse (modern)

Dangerous dragons

The Lambton Worm

Penshaw Hill in Tyne and Wear is the setting for a famous English dragon story, the Lambton Worm.

Hundreds of years ago, in the Middle Ages, the son and heir to the wealthy Lambton family went fishing in the nearby River Wear on a Sunday when he should have been in church. At the end of a bad day's fishing he had ended up with little else but an ugly worm-like creature which he threw into a well in disgust. The well was very near his home, Lambton Castle.

Some time after this, he decided to go off to fight on the Crusades in the Holy Land, but while he was away terrible things happened to the village. The worm he had thrown away, grew into a huge and hideous dragon, slithered out of the well and, to satisfy its hunger, raided the nearby farms and villages, killing sheep, cattle, pigs and even people.

The horrible beast seemed to be invincible. Although the bravest people in the village tried to kill it by cutting it in half, the beast's two ends joined up as if nothing had happened. At night, the dragon wound its horrible scaly body three times around a nearby hill (now known as Worm Hill, where you can see the ridges left by the sleeping dragon) and slept.

Seven years later the young man returned to find the villagers living in daily fear of the foul creature. He blamed himself for having caught the 'worm' in the first place and saw it as his duty to kill it.

Seeking the help of a witch, he found out a way to defeat the dragon. However the witch made him promise that in return for her help, he had to kill the first creature to greet him after his victory. If he didn't keep his part of the bargain the next nine generations of the Lambton family would not die peacefully. The young man agreed and the witch told him that the answer lay in simply covering his armour in razors and fighting the creature in the middle of the river.

On the day of the fight the young man did as the witch had told him. He also told his father that if he was successful, he would blow on his trumpet to let him know, but that his father must let loose a greyhound to meet him rather than running to the river himself. And so the young man stood in the middle of the river waiting for the awful creature. Sure enough it soon appeared. Breathing fire from its nostrils, it slunk into the river and began winding its horrible scaly body around the young man. But as it tightened its grip the dragon let out a terrible scream. The razors were cutting the creature into tiny pieces which were swept away by the river's current before they could rejoin the body. As the horrendous head floated away, the young man knew he had succeeded in his task and joyfully sounded his bugle.

His heart sank when he saw his father running to congratulate him. In his happiness and rush to see his son, the old man had forgotten the instructions. The son could not bring himself to kill his father, but from that day on the witch's curse took effect and for the next nine generations the Lambton family suffered as she had predicted.

The Nunnington Knight

Penshaw Hill isn't the only place to have been plagued with a magical, invincible dragon. A similar tale is told of Nunnington Hall in Yorkshire, where the dragon is defeated by a brave knight wearing razor armour, but this time it was his faithful dog who carried off the pieces of the monster before they could join together again.

Dragon Sites

In Old English the word for dragon was wurm. The headland off West Glamorgan is called Worm's Head because people thought that its shape looked like a dragon.

The ridges around Bignor Hill in West Sussex are said to be the marks of the coils left by a sleeping dragon. Dragons have certainly left their mark over our hills and coastline. Not all dragons, however, are British. According to folklore, Iceland is the body of a huge dragon called Meister Stoor Worm and the Faroe Islands are the monster's teeth.

The land of Arthur

Y ou may well have heard of King Arthur and Camelot, his magic sword, Excalibur, the Knights of the Round Table, the quest for the Holy Grail, the Wizard Merlin, Queen Guinevere and Sir Lancelot. But did you realise that no one really knows who, if anyone, Arthur was?

The most likely theory is that the stories sprung up around a successful Celtic leader, who fought off the invading Saxons from mainland Europe after the Romans left Britain at the beginning of the 5th century. With centuries of telling, the tales became more and more complicated until the legend of Arthur and his Knights of the Round Table was popular throughout the Western world. Many poets, painters, writers and film makers have given their version of the legend - even Walt Disney made a cartoon of the story.

King Arthur

According to legend, Arthur was born in the fifth century at Tintagel in Cornwall - the result of a trick played by King Uther Pendragon on Igerna, the wife of the Earl of Cornwall. With help from the Wizard Merlin, Pendragon disguised himself as Igerna's husband, crept into the castle and slept with her. Nine months later Igerna gave birth to a son, Arthur.

When he was 15 Arthur became king of the Britons by pulling a sword called Excalibur from a block of stone and steel marked with the words 'Whoso pulleth out this sword of this stone and anvil, is rightwise king born of all England'. Helped by the wizard Merlin he set up a court at Camelot with his queen Guinevere and the Knights of the Round Table, who vowed to live nobly and fight valiantly.

Arthur defeated the Saxons and was crowned emperor by the Pope, but things started to turn sour. Guinevere had an affair with Lancelot, Arthur's great friend, and civil war broke out between the two camps. After an order from the Pope, Lancelot agreed to give Guinevere back to Arthur and left the county for France to set up his own court.

Whoso pulleth out this sword of this stone and anvil, is rightwise king born of all England.

Arthur's Revenge

Arthur was determined to get revenge on his one-time friend and set sail across the Channel to fight. He left his nephew Mordred in charge of the kingdom, unaware that Mordred was in fact planning to betray him. While Arthur was in France, Mordred invented reports that Arthur had been killed in battle and persuaded the lords to crown him king. The tables were turned on Mordred when Arthur heard about the betrayal and returned to claim back his kingdom at the battle of Camlann. It was to be the King's last battle...

Arthur's Last Battle

The battle between Mordred and Arthur's troops raged long and hard all day. Many, many brave men had died on both sides, but as the day drew to a close it seemed that Arthur had succeeded in regaining his kingdom. However, Mordred was still alive and Arthur was determined to kill the traitor.

The pair locked themselves in a bloody combat – a fight to the death. Suddenly Mordred let out a blood-curdling cry as Arthur's sword sank into his body, but with one last supreme effort the traitor managed to lunge his sword at the King's head and strike a heavy blow. Mordred fell dead to the ground and Arthur collapsed exhausted and wounded, having accomplished his task.

Two faithful knights carried Arthur from the battlefield to the edge of a lake where the king commanded them to throw his magic sword, Excalibur, into the water. Reluctantly, they did as he asked and were astonished to see a hand rise from the lake, catch the sword and wave it three times before disappearing below the surface. Then, out of the mists, a stately barge approached them carrying three queens dressed in black. Without a word they took the body of the dying Arthur, gently laid him into the barge and drifted silently back into the mists.

Some people believe that Glastonbury Tor, a steep hill outside Glastonbury in Somerset, is the 'Fairy Isle of Avalon', where the dying Arthur was taken. Glastonbury Tor may well in fact have been an island in the age of Arthur as much of Somerset was then marshland. The belief is that the legendary King still lies sleeping in the hillside, but will wake and come to his country's aid if needed.

Glastonbury and the Grail

Glastonbury in Somerset has often been linked to Arthurian legend. It is said to be the location of the Holy Grail, the cup used at the Last Supper by Christ before the crucifixion. The Grail held the secret to eternal life and could only be found by a knight who was completely pure in heart. Arthur's Knights of the Round Table felt it was their mission to look for the missing Grail.

Arthur's Britain

Many other places in Britain claim to be connected with Arthur. Arthur's last and greatest victory over the Saxons was at the Battle of Mount Badon. Some think that Badbury Rings in Dorset is the site of this fight. Cadbury Castle, an Iron Age hill fort in Somerset, is thought by many to be Camelot, the court of King Arthur.

Arthurian Wordsearch

The Knights of the Round Table searched for the Holy Grail - can you find it and nine other words connected with the legend of Arthur in the grid?

G	L	A	S	T	O	N	B	U	R	Y
U	A	V	P	X	E	D	H	Y	F	R
I	B	A	B	O	X	C	O	E	W	O
N	R	L	A	N	C	E	L	O	T	U
I	Z	O	Q	L	A	E	Y	N	I	N
V	M	N	A	K	L	M	G	F	N	D
E	M	E	R	L	I	N	R	G	T	T
R	S	L	J	H	B	D	A	C	A	A
E	N	I	K	V	U	G	I	H	G	B
P	S	R	T	J	R	Q	L	O	E	L
M	O	D	R	E	D	I	G	V	L	E

Great escapes

S ome of the best escape stories come from the time of the English Civil War in the seventeenth century when the country was divided in two: the Cavaliers and Royalists supported the King, while the Roundheads and Puritans were led by Oliver Cromwell who wanted the abolition of the monarchy.

Look before you leap

On Wenlock Edge in Staffordshire is a spot known as Major's Leap. During the Civil War Major Thomas Smallman - a Cavalier - was being kept prisoner in his own home, Wilderhope Manor. He escaped and was pursued by Roundhead soldiers on to Wenlock Edge - Smallman saw nothing for it but to ride his horse over the edge - his horse died, but Smallman's fall was broken by a tree and he survived, leaving his Roundhead pursuers stranded. The spot has been known as Major's Leap ever since. This is quite a common story - there are various 'Leaps' around the country. Another one is on the cliffs above the River Wye in Gloucestershire, known as Wintour's Leap. In the West country in Cornwall stands Bodrugan's Leap which dates back to Tudor times.

A king in a tight spot

One of the most famous escape tales concerns King Charles II. After his defeat at the battle of Worcester in 1651, he had to use a range of disguises and the help of his loyal subjects to flee the country. Amongst other places he hid in a priest hole at Moseley Old Hall, in Staffordshire, in a false wall between two bedrooms, with an entrance through the floor leading to a secret hiding place. His most famous hiding place, however, was up an oak tree in the grounds of Boscobel House where he spent an entire night while Roundhead troops searched the area.

Packed in

At Baddesley Clinton House in Warwickshire, there is a priest hole built into the drains underneath the kitchen where nine men hid and escaped capture in 1591.

Tall tales

Sometimes 'true' stories get exaggerated the more they are told. In the sixteenth century Olive Sharrington, the daughter of the owner of Lacock Abbey in Wiltshire, became secretly engaged to her lover, John Talbot, but was sure her family would never allow her to marry him. She decided to take drastic measures and run away to join him by jumping off the Abbey battlements.

Olive's petticoats turned into a makeshift parachute and slowed her descent, but unfortunately her fiancé bore the brunt of the fall and was almost killed when she landed on top of him! Olive's father was so impressed by her display of love that he agreed to her marrying Talbot when he had recovered from his injuries.

Can the Roundheads find the priest?

Secret hide-outs

During Britain's history there have been many times when people have been persecuted for their religious beliefs. In the Tudor and Stuart age, Protestants or Catholics were persecuted in turn depending who was on the throne. As a result, many old families who lived in stately homes found themselves practising their version of Christianity in secret. Under Elizabeth I, Catholic priests were in particular danger and many houses had secret compartments and rooms built to hide them from the authorities - these hideaways were naturally known as priest holes.

Larger than life

Throughout the ages, tales have sprung up around famous people and in time have become so exaggerated that the hero is turned into a legendary figure, capable of amazing and often magical powers. One such person was Sir Francis Drake, the celebrated sixteenth-century naval leader and explorer.

Devilish Drake

Drake masterminded the defeat of the Spanish navy which tried to invade England in 1588. He spent much of his life at sea raiding Spanish treasure ships. The Spaniards were so in awe of his talents that they believed that Drake had sold his soul to the Devil in return for a supernatural skill of seafaring. They even believed he had a magic mirror in which he could trace the movements of ships all over the world's oceans.

Drumming up support

Drake's home base for the last sixteen years of his life was Buckland Abbey in Devon. You can visit this converted monastery and see many items connected with Drake, including a drum rumoured to have magical qualities. It is said that if ever England is in danger the drum should be beaten and Sir Francis Drake will come back from the dead to save his country once more. Legend has it that the drum rolled of its own accord before the battle of Trafalgar, in 1805, and that when the German fleet officially surrendered to the British at Scapa Flow in 1918, a mysterious drum beat was heard on the British flagship but no drummer could be found.

Drake's Canon-ball

Sir Francis Drake was born into a poor family but through his skill in seafaring, he became one of the most famous men in Elizabethan England. After his first wife died, Drake married Elizabeth Sydenham, a local beauty from an old Somerset aristocratic family. Although the Sydenham family had let the marriage take place, they were not completely happy with Drake's humble roots and would have preferred Elizabeth to marry someone from a similar aristocratic background.

Drake continued his life of exploration and raiding Spanish treasure ships but on one trip was away far longer than he had promised to Elizabeth. The days and months and years went by and still there was no sign of her husband. Finally her parents came to her and said "Francis will never come back - he has been away for too long. You shouldn't waste your life waiting for a dead man to return - you are still young, why not marry again?" But Elizabeth refused and every day walked to the cliffs gazing at the horizon, straining her eyes for a sign of her husband's ship returning.

Another year passed and her parents came to her again, suggesting the name of a suitable husband from a good family. With a heavy heart, Elizabeth finally agreed that Francis must be dead and consented to the marriage. However, a sea spirit overheard the conversation and, knowing Drake was still alive, swam swiftly through the oceans of the world to find the explorer and tell him what was happening.

At last, the spirit found Drake stuck in the doldrums in the Pacific Ocean, thousands of miles away. The exhausted spirit explained about Elizabeth's marriage and without delay, the horrified

Dead Chuffed

When Drake died some people couldn't believe that he had really gone and a rumour spread that he had turned into a rare Cornish bird, the Chough, and could be seen flying around the West Country coast.

Drake fired a cannon-ball high up into the sky. "Now she will know that I am alive" he said as it disappeared into the distance.

Back in Somerset, Elizabeth was starting to walk down the church aisle towards her new husband. Suddenly there was an enormous crash and sound of splintering wood as a cannon-ball thundered through the roof and landed bang in front of the bride-to-be. In the commotion Elizabeth started laughing with joy, shouting "It is a sign, Francis is coming back to me" and ran out of the church, leaving her groom standing at the altar. Sure enough, several months later, Drake's ship appeared over the horizon and the happy couple were reunited.

The 'cannon-ball' which stopped Elizabeth marrying is kept at the Sydenham family home in Somerset. It has been identified as a meteorite.

Mariners and Miners

Humans have never really conquered the sea and people who live by the coast or make their living on the ocean have many tales to tell of the great power of the seas and the secrets of their watery depths.

It was said that seals could shed their skins and become humans, and that they often came ashore at night to sing and dance on the beach. If a man could steal the skin of a seal maiden she had to stay with him until she was given her skin back. One clan in the Outer Hebrides of Scotland is known as the Offspring of the Seals because a distant descendant is said to have married a seal maiden who bore him many children.

Animal or person?

A modern explanation for the existence of 'mermaids' is the sea-cow or dugong. This large seal-like creature is rumoured to be able to transfix humans and beckon them out to sea and if seen basking on a rock could perhaps be mistaken for a woman with a fish tail. There are very recent tales of deep sea divers becoming fascinated by dugongs and almost being led to their deaths, following this strange creature to the depths of the ocean.

Underwater singing

Zennor church in Cornwall has a pew end carved with the figure of a mermaid, a reminder of the local legend of a chorister in the church choir who had such a beautiful voice that a mermaid fell in love with it - she tempted him into the sea and he was never seen again. It is said that his voice can still be heard wafting up from the waves.

Stiff as a Statue

Mariners were very superstitious people. Frederick Hervey was the Bishop of Derry and owner of Ickworth House in Suffolk. He spent much of his time travelling abroad. When he fell ill and died on one of his trips in 1803, his body was preserved, boxed up and sent back to England by sea labelled as an 'Antique Statue'. Sailors were so superstitious they would have considered it very bad luck to travel with a dead body on board.

Holy Island

Lindisfarne, also known as Holy Island, off the coast of Northumberland, was where St Cuthbert, a 7th-century monk, spent most of his life. He was famous for his love of birds and animals and one story tells how, after a night spent praying standing in the freezing cold North Sea, he knelt down on the shore and a pair of seals came up to dry his feet with their fur and warm them with their breath.

Look for pebbles on the beach at Lindisfarne and see if you can find one of 'St Cuthbert's beads'. These are stones with a hole worn by the sea in the centre and if hung on a chain will bring good luck to the wearer and protect him or her from drowning.

Mining lore

Miners, like sailors and fishermen, had many superstitions connected to their dangerous job. Crows, red-headed women and howling dogs were all considered to foretell disaster. The tin miners of Cornwall and the lead miners of Wales believed in invisible spirits, called Knockers, who lived underground in the mines and could bring good luck by leading the miners to rich seams of ore by the sound of their tapping. Some believed them to be the spirits of Jews who crucified Christ and were forced to work underground as a punishment; others held them to be a race of people who lived in Cornwall before the Celts and were neither good enough for heaven nor bad enough for hell. If a miner was helped by the Knockers he had to make sure to reward them by leaving out food or else bad luck would plague him.

Bad omens

If, on his way to work, a miner met someone with a squint, or his path was crossed by a rabbit or bird, he should go home for the day. If people dreamt of disaster or death or if there were strange omens, it was thought best to avoid going down the pit the next day.

This belief in superstition appeared to have saved the lives of many miners at the Morfa Colliery near Port Talbot in Wales on 10 March 1890. There had been many spooky happenings the day before: eerie cries for help and sounds of falling earth had been heard in the mine; ghosts of dead miners had been seen; rats swarmed out of the pit and a sweet rose-like smell filled the tunnels.

Nearly half the miners decided to stay at home the following day and sure enough an explosion in the afternoon caused the deaths of 87 miners who had braved the omens and gone down the mine.

Ghosts and ghoulies

There are many ghost stories surrounding National Trust properties, covering just about every kind of ghoul, from Roman times to the twentieth century. Some ghosts have never been seen but their eerie presence is said to have been felt, whilst others just leave a smell, and some can only be heard. There is even a story of a phantom motorbike.

Devilish Drives

Not surprisingly, it is said that Sir Francis Drake's ghost haunts Dartmoor in Devon. He is said to drive across the moor in a black coach drawn by four headless horses, following twelve horrible goblins with a pack of baying hounds following him. Any dog who hears the howling of the ghostly dogs dies instantly. This story probably came about from the rumours that Drake had sold his soul to the Devil in exchange for unearthly seafaring skills.

Half-hearted hauntings

You may think that headless ghosts are quite common, but have you ever heard of footless ones? Some very special legless ghosts have been spotted many times at the Treasurer's House in York, a building on the site of part of the Via Decumana, an ancient Roman Road.

In the 1950's, a young plumber called Harry Martindale had been called to do some work in the basement cellar of Treasurer's House. It was dark and a little spooky so he busied himself getting on with his job. As he was knocking a hole through one wall he stopped, thinking that he heard the sound of a trumpet in the distance, gradually getting louder and louder. Harry couldn't think where the noise was coming from. He turned round and was amazed to see a figure of a Roman soldier appearing THROUGH the opposite wall, followed by a horse ridden by another Roman legionary.

As the astonished plumber stared in disbelief he saw a whole troop of soldiers trudge across the cellar floor and disappear through the wall on the opposite side. They wore plain clothes but carried round shields, long spears and wore plumed helmets. The strange thing was that they were only visible from the knee upwards until they reached the part of the cellar where archaeologists had been working and the floor had been dug down eighteen inches to the original Roman road, then Harry could see their legs right down to their feet.

As the last soldier disappeared through the wall, the white-faced young man ran upstairs and blurted his extraordinary tale out to the curator of the house. In fact the man was not particularly surprised as he was well aware of the story of the mysterious legion but told Harry that he was the only person ever to have seen the feet of the ghostly soldiers.

Mystery Monks

Fountains Abbey, a huge ruined twelfth-century monastery in North Yorkshire is said to have a phantom choir of monks which has been heard chanting in the Chapel of the Nine Altars.

By Royal Appointment

Blickling Hall in Norfolk is also rumoured to have a royal ghost. The present house is built on the site of Anne Boleyn's birthplace. Anne was Henry VIII's second wife and was executed on Henry's orders in 1536. It is said that on the night of her execution, 19th May, she comes back to Blickling driven in a coach pulled by headless horses and driven by a headless coachman. Other sightings have always mentioned that she wears a long grey dress with a white collar and mob cap - which fits the description of the clothes which she wore on the day of her death.

Scents of the past ...

The tea-room at Emmetts Garden in Kent has a very unusual ghost - a horse. The old stables were converted into the tea-room and one of the old inmates obviously decided to stay around... Sometimes the horse can be heard kicking the wall at the far end bay while other times visitors are put off their tea and scones by a horsey smell as the ghost walks past.

Other pongy ghosts can be found at Blickling Hall in Norfolk where there is often a mysterious lingering smell of violets. This is said to be the spirit of the wife of the 2nd Earl of Buckinghamshire who was a country-loving person and made her own perfume out of wild violets.

A helping hand

During the Civil War in the seventeenth century, Sir Edmund Verney of Claydon House, Buckinghamshire fought for the Royalists and was King Charles I's standard bearer. At the battle of Edgehill in 1642 he was captured by the Roundheads but refused to let go of the standard. The enemy cut off his hand, still gripping the flag, and killed the loyal bearer. Later on in the battle the Royalists regained the Standard and, according to legend, with Sir Edmund's hand still gripping it. The hand was taken back to Claydon and buried but his body was never found and it is said that the ghost of Sir Edmund haunts Claydon looking for his lost hand.

Brrrm, brrrm!

A relatively modern ghost is said to haunt Clouds Hill in Dorset, the home of the famous explorer, Lawrence of Arabia. Lawrence was killed in a motorbike accident in 1935 when driving home to his cottage. On some nights the ghostly roar of a phantom motorbike can be heard in the lanes near the cottage.

Ghostly howlers

What happens to actors in a haunted theatre?

They get stage fright

What do ghosts eat?

Spookghetti

What's a ghost's favourite ride at the funfair?

The roller ghoster

Spooky Springhill

The ghost of Olivia Lenox-Conyngham is said to appear only to young people and children at Springhill House in Co. Londonderry, Northern Ireland. Although Olivia herself died a natural death, her husband committed suicide and her daughter died young and she is said still to wander the corridors of Springhill House.

Your money or your life

George and Joseph Weston were apparently respectable eighteenth-century gentlemen living in the Sussex town of Winchelsea but at night they took on a different role and became highwaymen terrorising the roads. Their downfall came one night in 1782 when they tried to hold up the Bristol mail coach and were captured and hanged for their crime. However, the Westons are still seen around their old haunts, and motorists have reported hearing the sound of phantom galloping hooves at night.

Ghostly writing

You can surprise your friends by making ghostly writing appear from nowhere.

You need:

a sheet of plain white paper

a clear wax crayon

water colour paint

Write your secret message using the wax crayon and then paint over it with a dark colour and see the message magically appear.

Superstitions

Everyone knows that it's supposed to be bad luck if you walk under a ladder, or break a mirror, but did you realise .....

At Halloween a girl can see who she is to marry if she looks in the mirror. If she wants more detail she can throw a complete apple peel over her shoulder - it will land and form the initial of her husband-to-be.

It is unlucky to bring hawthorn into the house before May Day.

To make sure bread will rise you should cut a cross in the top of the dough to 'let the Devil out'.

It is said that a very ill person will recover as long as he or she lies on a mattress or pillow stuffed with dove feathers.

It is bad luck to drink from a jug.

Some medicinal cures are distinctly dubious ....

To get rid of warts you should count how many you have and then put the same number of pebbles into a bag. Then take the bag to a cross-roads and leave it there. The first person to pick up the bag will get your warts.

If you get bitten by a mad dog you should hold the key of a church door and it will protect you from any harm.

Some 'cures' were worse than the illness ...
A dead mole hung around the neck protects the wearer from toothache.

Malicious Magpies

You have probably heard the rhyme about magpies which starts -

'One for sorrow, two for joy,

Three for a girl and four for a boy'

It is meant to be very unlucky to see a single magpie; there are several ways to get rid of the bad luck:

some make the sign of the cross;

others say 'I salute you, Sir Magpie'.

In Somerset it used to be the custom to carry an onion in your pocket to protect you from the magpie's curse!

A cat weathervane

If a cat sneezes, or washes its ears, it is going to rain.

If it claws at curtains and carpets there will be a strong wind.

Weird and wonderful beasts

In the Middle Ages the world as we know it was still largely unexplored and people believed that far-off lands were populated with monsters and strange creatures. 'Bestiaries' became popular - these were beautifully illustrated books describing all manner of fabulous beasts. Most of the creatures - some real and others mythical - were said to have strange powers, such as the panther whose breath was so sweet that it attracted its prey, or the mythical Amphisbaena, a weird poisonous reptile with a head at each end of its body. Although you won't find any living mythical beasts like these in National Trust properties, keep a close look out and see some of them used in heraldry or in decoration in the houses and gardens.

Coats of Arms

The unicorn, together with the lion, is one of the supporters on the Royal Coat of Arms. The unicorn was said to be a sacred beast symbolising purity and virtue. It also features on the coat of arms of Sir Edward Dalyngrigge who built Bodiam Castle in Sussex in the fourteenth century.

Here are a few more animals featured in heraldry at other National Trust properties.

Glorious griffins

The griffin is the king of mythical beasts with the body of a lion and the head and wings of an eagle. You can see statues of griffins on the terrace at Polesden Lacey in Surrey and there are also four mysterious griffin heads on the lawn at Wallington in Northumberland.

Shugborough Seahorses (Staffordshire)

One of the supporters is a seahorse. The Anson family had a great seafaring tradition and used the seahorse to stress this maritime connection.

The Verney Phoenix (Claydon House, Buckinghamshire)

You can see the phoenix incorporated on the top left of this family's shield - a mythical bird which grew to a great age then died in a blaze of fire, from which a new young phoenix rose from the ashes.

Other strange creatures to look out for:

Wyverns - you'll find these strange scaly birdlike creatures throughout Claydon House in Buckinghamshire

Dodos - at Mount Stewart in Northern Ireland you can see four statues of this extinct bird on the Dodo terrace in the garden.

Eagrot at The Vyne

The Vyne in Hampshire has an accidental mythological creature. At its entrance stand two stone birds. They were originally both eagles but in the nineteenth century one head was damaged and sent away for repair. The stonemason was obviously not an ornithologist as the damaged eagle was returned with the beak of a parrot!

Mad about Mermaids

Robert Adam, the famous eighteenth-century architect and designer, was particularly fond of using mythical creatures in his designs. If you visit Kedleston Hall in Derbyshire you can see a set of sofas which he designed where the legs and arms are in the form of merfolk - mermen and mermaids.

Make your own bestiary

Mix and match one word from the first column with one from the second (e.g. Penpard - mixture of a penguin and a leopard).
Then draw what you imagine the creature would look like with a description of its behaviour and powers.

Ele	phant
Kanga	roo
Ante	lope
Leo	pard
Peli	can
Don	key
Pen	guin

Eye of newt and toe of frog...

The Wizard of Cwyrtycadno

A famous wizard lived in Wales, in a cottage now owned by the National Trust. Dr John Harries was known throughout Wales for his magical powers and people came from all over the country for his help. Among his many talents were curing illnesses, foretelling the future, overcoming witchcraft and being able to discover missing objects. He died in 1839.

The Wizard of Alderley Edge

One fine day a farmer from Mobberley in Cheshire decided that he would take his best white mare to Macclesfield market to sell her for a good price.

As he rode along Alderley Edge on the magnificent beast he began to daydream about what he would buy with the money from the sale. Then he suddenly stopped dead in his tracks. There, blocking his way, was the strangest man he'd ever seen - a figure with a snow white beard down to his waist and wearing a long cloak of the deepest blue imaginable.

"What do you want?" asked the mystified farmer. "I want to buy your horse" replied the old man. "I will give you this purse of money for her." The farmer looked suspiciously at the bag and said "I know I will get twice that at market. Let me pass." Stepping aside, the wizard let the man go on his way.

Later that morning the farmer arrived at Macclesfield and many people came up to him and enquired about the horse but at the end of the day the farmer had not received a single firm offer for his prized mare. Disappointed, he trudged his way home, with his head hung low, kicking himself for not taking up the wizard's offer in the first place. But when he reached Alderley Edge, the farmer's path was blocked once again by the white-haired old man.

Without speaking a word, the wizard beckoned him to follow and the farmer was led to a cave barred with iron gates. With a wave of the wizard's wand, the gates creaked open and, to his amazement, the farmer saw that the cavern was filled with sleeping soldiers and horses. The wizard turned to him and said "We need just one more horse", pointing at a lone slumbering soldier. "If ever England is in danger this army will wake up and help but until we find a horse to complete the cavalry we will not be able to do so."

The farmer was so amazed at the sight that he grabbed the wizard's purse and ran out of the enchanted cave leaving the white mare behind. Although in years to come he went back to the ridge many times to look for the iron-barred cave, the farmer never found any trace of it, or the wizard, again.

The wizard's well

On another Alderley Edge in Shropshire you will find a naturally formed well with the message

'Drink of this and take thy fill,

For the water falls by the wizard's will.'

No-win situation

The sixteenth and seventeenth centuries in Europe were a terrifying period of witch-hunting when thousands of innocent people were sent to their deaths because it was 'proved' that they were witches. One popular way of finding out whether a woman was a witch or not was to tie the suspect up and duck her in a pond: if she floated it was proof that she was a witch and she would be hanged or burnt at the stake - if she sank she was 'proved' innocent but usually drowned in the process.

One of the most famous English witch hunters was called Matthew Hopkins. From 1645-6 he carried out a ruthless quest to rid East Anglia of 'witches' claiming that he had the Devil's list naming them all. His method was to find the 'Devil's mark' on the body of the suspect - this could be anything from a mole, insect bite or wart - and then force a confession by torture. As most of his victims were frail, old women they would often confess to extraordinary things just to stop the torture. In his reign of terror it is thought that Hopkins was responsible for the death of about four hundred 'witches'.

The Wizard Earl

Petworth in Sussex had its own 'wizard' during the 16th and 17th centuries. The 9th Earl of Northumberland, Henry Percy (1564-1632) was the owner of the Petworth Estate and was keen on science. He was particularly keen on the Elizabethan science of alchemy - studying how to turn ordinary metals into gold and to search for eternal life. For his strange experiments he gained the nickname of the 'Wizard Earl'.

Grisly gossip

Beware, wicked stepmother!

King Edward the Martyr was killed on the site of Corfe Castle in Dorset in 978 - a murder said to have been planned by his stepmother who wanted to put his half-brother, Ethelred on the throne. The unsuspecting Edward was stabbed while on a visit to the castle and his body was thrown down a well. However, a ray of light beamed out of the hole and led people to find the body of the murdered king. His body was taken for burial at Shaftesbury. A cult then grew up around the murdered king and miracles were said to take place at the site of his tomb.

Bad reputation

Edward's murder isn't the only nasty thing to have taken place at Corfe Castle. 'Bad' King John imprisoned his niece, Eleanor, at Corfe for nearly ten years at the beginning of the twelfth century. While she herself was treated quite well, her twenty-five French knights imprisoned with her were brutally treated. After a failed escape attempt the knights were punished so severely that 22 of them died from starvation.

A strange cure for aching teeth

In 1791 William Winter was hanged for murder and the gibbet on which he died is still standing on Wallington Estate in Northumberland, with a model of his body hanging from the noose. There is a local belief that if you have toothache and take a splinter of wood from the gibbet and rub it on your gum, the toothache will be cured.

Hungry ghosts

Bramber Castle in Sussex is haunted by the sad ghosts of three children of the Norman lord, William de Breose. King John was wary of William and imprisoned his three children as hostages, starving them to death in their own home. The ghostly children are seen begging for scraps of food outside the castle walls.

A skeleton in the cupboard

In 1872, at Ightham Mote in Kent, builders doing restoration work to the panelling found a skeleton of a young girl bricked up in a cupboard.

A Deadly Package

In 1665 the Great Plague raged through London. Once a person caught the plague it was almost certain that he or she would die and the disease, which was carried by fleas, was very contagious.

The little village of Eyam in Derbyshire was miles away from the disease-infected capital, but in the autumn of 1665 tragedy struck when the village tailor was delivered a packet of cloth from London. As the man opened up the package he had no idea that he was letting the deadly plague loose in the village. Hiding in the cloth were some of the fatal disease-carrying fleas.

Within two days the poor tailor developed the tell-tale symptoms - swellings, a rash and a raging fever. Within a week the tailor was dead and others were falling ill at an alarming rate. The vicar, the Rev. William Mompesson, realising that the terrible disease would

spread like wildfire, managed to persuade his parishioners that, even though they themselves were probably doomed, they should do all they could to stop the plague spreading outside the village.

From that day onwards the people of Eyam shut themselves off from the outside world. No one left the village and no-one was allowed in. One by one the villagers fell ill and died, until only eighty three people out of the original population of three hundred and fifty were left. But even though the death toll was high, hundreds, maybe thousands of lives in the neighbouring villages and towns, had been saved by the unselfish attitude of the people of Eyam.

If you visit this part of Derbyshire you can see a sad reminder of this tragedy. The Riley graves, on a hillside outside Eyam, mark the spot where seven members of the Hancock family were buried in a single week.

An ill-fated mill

Park Mill, at Bateman's in Sussex, has two gruesome legends connected to it. Years ago the miller was an old miser and stories of his hoard of gold were well known. One night, having heard of the riches hidden away in the mill, a masked robber broke in, stabbed the miller and escaped with the gold.

The other sad story tells of a miller's daughter running away with her lover, only to fall through some rotting planks on the bridge into the Dudwell river, where the unlucky pair drowned.

Stains that won't budge

At Cotehele in Cornwall, the story goes that a man was murdered near the entrance to the house and that in spite of hours of scrubbing, the 'bloodstains' could not be removed from the flagstones.

What the devil...

Many features of the landscape have been given strange names. Sometimes the reason is obvious, other times there can be a complicated tale behind the title. Some rock formations on the North Yorkshire Moors are called the Salt Cellar and Pepper Pot while if you visit Dovedale, Derbyshire you'll find the Twelve Apostles and Jacob's Ladder. However, many of Britain's place names are not quite so holy and in fact you'll find the Devil cropping up all over the place .....

Devil's Dyke

The Devil was particularly fond of living it up on Saturday nights on the South Downs but got extremely annoyed on Sunday mornings when the local villagers, who insisted on getting up early for church and ringing the bells, did not do a lot for his hangover.

One night the Devil decided he had enough and decided to put an end to the troublesome villagers forever by flooding the whole parish. His plan was to dig a ditch from the South Downs to the coast which would let the sea water sweep in, stopping the bell-ringing once and for all. Pulling huge lumps of earth from the ground, the Devil set to work throwing the clods over his shoulder as he went. The noise of his activity woke an old woman in a nearby farmhouse who lit a candle in her window to see what was going on. Over his shoulder the Devil caught a glimpse of the light, thought it was the rising sun and that dawn had come and that it was time to get back to hell, so he dropped what he was doing and ran off to the inferno. The villagers were saved and the unfinished ditch he left is known as Devil's Dyke.

Devil's Night-cap

While sitting on the Needles (see below) in the Isle of Wight, the Devil decided that he didn't like the look of Corfe Castle in Dorset and threw his night-cap at it - he missed and his hat landed outside Studland, miles off target. It turned into stone and is known as the Devil's Night-cap.

Devil's Grave

On Wenlock Edge in Shropshire lies a strange rectangular block of stone. People say that it marks the grave of the Devil.

Other devilish names to look out for:

Devil's Cauldron

Devil's Elbow

Devil's Punchbowl

Devil's Jumps

Devil's Bridge

The Needles

Off the Isle of Wight you can see the Needles where the Devil sat - a series of three sharp chalk outcrops standing up from the sea, separated from the cliffs as a result of the erosion of the soft chalk by the pounding waves. There used to be four Needles, but the tallest crumbled into the sea in 1764 - it was called Lot's wife after the Biblical story of a woman who was turned into a pillar of salt.

Attention, missing saint!

At Dolaucothi Gold Mines in South Wales, stands a strange rock called the Five Saint's Stone (or in Welsh, Carreg Pumsaint). The story goes that five saints rested against it one night and each left a dent where he lay his head. The only problem is that there are four dents ...

Travel game

If you're travelling look out for odd-sounding place names on road signs. Make up a story about how the place got its name.

29

Strange tails

The Grave of Gelert

In North Wales is a little village called Beddgelert, with a 'long tail' behind its name. The Welsh name means 'grave of Gelert' and true enough if you visit you can see a cairn (or pile of stones) which is said to mark the spot where Gelert, the faithful dog of a thirteenth-century Welsh prince, is buried. There is, however, a shaggy dog's tale behind its name.

Prince Llewellyn trusted his dog so completely that he was happy to leave Gelert baby-sitting his young baby son while he went out. One day Llewellyn went out hunting leaving Gelert in charge and a hungry wolf entered the room and tried to attack the baby boy. Gelert bravely fought the wolf off and after a fierce fight the wolf lay dying in the corner. Exhausted and covered with blood Gelert took guard of the baby again. Tragedy struck when Prince Llewellyn returned and saw his faithful dog smeared in blood and jumped to the conclusion that Gelert had attacked and killed his son. In his anger he took his sword and killed Gelert instantly. The commotion woke the sleeping baby and Llewellyn, hardly believing his ears, ran to the cradle to see his son safe and sound. Then he saw the body of the huge wolf lying on the floor and realised what a terrible mistake he'd made and that he had killed the very animal who'd saved his son's life.

This story of a faithful dog killed by his master was a popular theme of folklore, and was adapted in this case by an eighteenth-century local inn keeper who wanted to attract more people to the area - and his pub. He sold his story to a ballad writer and the tragic tale of Gelert soon spread throughout the land, encouraging visitors to flood to the village to visit the brave dog's 'grave'.

The Magical Poodle

During the English Civil Wars, one of the most daring commanders on the Royalist side was Prince Rupert of the Rhine. The Roundheads suspected that his pet poodle, Boy, was a magic animal as he always went into battle with Rupert. They were overjoyed when the dog, known as the 'shagged cavalier', was shot dead in 1644 at the Battle of Marston Moor.

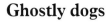

Here lyeth the faithful GELERT R.I.P.

Ghostly dogs

Dartmoor is said to have a ghostly hound which roams its eerie landscape. This is where Arthur Conan Doyle got his inspiration for his famous Sherlock Holmes mystery, *The Hound of the Baskervilles*.

Magical Mythstery Tour

The National Trust protects historic houses, gardens, coast and countryside throughout England, Wales and Northern Ireland. Some of the tales you have read are mapped out for you on the 'mythstery' tour on this page. Look closely at the map - can you match the drawings up with the myths and legends and the different places they are associated with? See if you can add some more.

You may one day come across different versions of the stories you have read in these pages, so you will be able to see how tales are changed as they are passed on to us. You may have your own local legends, to add to these National Trust tales, or you, as a story teller, have the power to add to or change a local tale for your own audience.

National Trust Places to Visit

Alderley Edge, Cheshire

Avebury, Wiltshire

Badbury Rings, Dorset

Baddesley Clinton, Warwickshire

Bateman's, Sussex

Buckland Abbey, Devon

Carn Galver, Cornwall

Cerne Giant, Dorset

Clouds Hill, Dorset

Corfe Castle, Dorset

Cotehele, Cornwall

Dolaucothi Gold Mines, South Wales

Fountains Abbey, Yorkshire

Giant's Causeway, Northern Ireland

Ickworth, Suffolk

Ightham Mote, Kent

Kedleston Hall, Derbyshire

Knole, Kent

Lacock Abbey, Wiltshire

Lindisfarne, Northumberland

Moseley Old Hall, Staffordshire

Mount Stewart, Northern Ireland

Needles Old Battery, Isle of Wight

Nunnington Hall, Yorkshire

Petworth, Sussex

St Michael's Mount, Cornwall

Speke Hall, Merseyside

Tintagel Old Post Office, Cornwall

Treasurer's House, York

The Vyne, Hampshire

Wenlock Edge, Shropshire

Worm's Head, West Glamorgan

Zennor, Cornwall

Answers

p.11 Arthurian Wordsearch

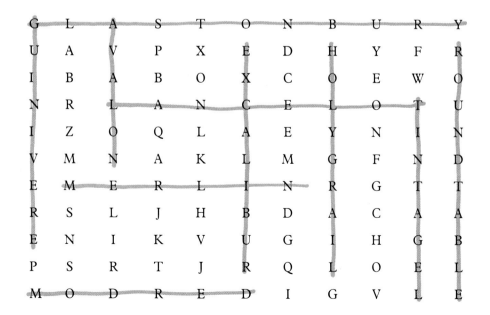

First published in 1994 by National Trust (Enterprises) Ltd, 36 Queen Anne's Gate, London SW1H 9AS

Registered Charity No. 205846

Copyright © The National Trust 1994

Reprinted 1998

ISBN: 0-7078-0180-X

Designed by Blade Communications, Leamington Spa

Printed by Wing King Tong Ltd., Hong Kong